AN INT
QL MA

ALSO BY THE SAME AUTHORS

AN INTRODUCTION TO
QL MACHINE CODE

by

R. A. & J. W. PENFOLD

**BERNARD BABANI (publishing) LTD
THE GRAMPIANS
SHEPHERDS BUSH ROAD
LONDON W6 7NF
ENGLAND**

PLEASE NOTE

Although every care has been taken with the production of this book to ensure that any projects, designs, modifications and/or programs etc. contained herein, operate in a correct and safe manner and also that any components specified are normally available in Great Britain, the Publishers do not accept responsibility in any way for the failure, including fault in design, of any project, design, modification or program to work correctly or to cause damage to any other equipment that it may be connected to or used in conjunction with, or in respect of any other damage or injury that may be so caused, nor do the Publishers accept responsibility in any way for the failure to obtain specified components.

Notice is also given that if equipment that is still under warranty is modified in any way or used or connected with home-built equipment then that warranty may be void.

All the programs and information in this book have been written and tested by the Authors using a number of production models of the QL that were available in Great Britain at the time of writing. However, as Sinclair Research Ltd have a policy of constant development and improvement of their products it is possible that details of hardware, software and/or firmware could be modified in the future.

Details of the graphics modes may vary with versions of the machine for other countries.

© 1985 BERNARD BABANI (publishing) LTD

First Published — March 1985

British Library Cataloguing in Publication Data:
Penfold, R.A.
    An introduction to QL machine code. — (BP.156)
    1. Sinclair QL (Microcomputer) — Programming
    2. Machine codes (Electronic computers)
    I. Title   II. Penfold, J.W.
    001.64'24   QA76.8.S625

    ISBN 0 85934 131 3

Printed and bound in Great Britain by Cox & Wyman Ltd, Reading.

PREFACE

From the machine code programmer's point of view the Sinclair QL computer is a very attractive proposition, offering access to the extremely powerful 68008 microprocessor at low cost. With its 32 bit registers, large address range, and advanced range of instructions which include such things as multiplication and division, this microprocessor is a step forward from the 8 bit microprocessors used in most home computers. Although one might think that an advanced microprocessor would be rather difficult for a beginner to program, this is not really the case. In fact the advanced specification of the 68008 makes many programming tasks much more simple than when using one of the standard 8 bit types. It is therefore possible for a beginner to run simple machine code programs on the QL, and to understand the way in which they function, after a few microprocessor fundamentals have been mastered. This book assumes no previous knowledge of either the 68008 or machine code programming, and takes the reader through to the stage where he or she should be able to design and run simple machine code programs. A few simple demonstration programs are included in the final section of this book.

R.A. & J.W. Penfold

CONTENTS

Chapter 1

THE MICROPROCESSOR

All home-computers are equipped to operate using a high level computer language such as BASIC or FORTH, and these languages are designed to make program design as quick and easy as possible. With most high level languages, including the QL's Sinclair Super-BASIC, the programmer uses words that are virtually plain English, and the computer's built-in software then converts these into machine code routines that the microprocessor at the heart of the computer can interpret and act upon. Writing programs direct in machine code is, on the face of it, rather pointless, as it is somewhat harder and a considerably slower process than using Sinclair Super-BASIC or another high level language to achieve the same ends.

The advantage of machine code programs is the speed with which they run. The speed of a machine code program is, in fact, only limited by the operating speed of the computer's microprocessor, and a computer can perform no faster than when it is running a machine code program. High level languages such as Sinclair Super-BASIC are inevitably much slower due to the way in which each instruction has to first be interpretted (converted into machine code) before it can be executed. In other words, the program is stored in memory in its Super-BASIC form, and it is only when the program is run that each instruction is converted into machine code and executed. The program is effectively brought to halt during the interpreting process, which accounts for more time than the running of the interpretted machine code. The difference in speed is probably much greater than most people realise, and machine code is typically something approaching one thousand times faster than an equivalent BASIC program. Action games written in any form of BASIC are usually a little sluggish due to this lack of operating speed, especially when a lot starts to happen at once, but a machine code equivalent normally appears to operate instantly no matter how much simultaneous action takes place. With some scientific and business programs BASIC is too slow to be of

1

any use at all, and the use of machine code is mandatory. However, the speed of machine code is its only advantage, and apart (perhaps) for the fun of it, there is no point in using machine code where a program written in a high level language would be fast enough.

There are alternatives to machine code and high level interpretted languages such as BASIC, and we will consider these briefly before moving on to a description of the microprocessor itself. Some high level languages are compiled rather than interpretted. The difference is that with a compiled language the interpreting process is carried out before the program is run. The program may then run using the compiled machine code, or using a sort of pseudo machine code which requires a mimimal amount of interpreting. In either case programs should run at high speed, and should be far easier to write than equivalent machine code programs. A compiled language may seem like the ideal solution (and many people would argue that it is), but languages of this type are generally much more difficult to use than interpretted languages when writing and debugging programs, and languages such as BASIC are probably much better for beginners to programming. A mixture of BASIC and machine code (with the latter only being used where high operating speed is essential) can therefore be a more practical solution in many cases.

Incidentally, you may come across the terms source code and object code occasionally. The former is the program in its high level language form, and the latter is the machine code or pseudo machine code produced after interpretation or compilation.

Assembly Language

The terms machine code and assembly language seem to cause a certain amount of confusion, and there seems to be a general belief that they are different terms for the same thing. In fact they are very similar, but there is an important difference. When machine code programming, the instructions for the microprocessor are in the form of numbers which are usually from 0 to 255, but in the case of the QL's advanced 68008 microprocessor the numbers are from 0 to 65535. In fact some instructions require more than one code number. This is not a very convenient way of doing things, and it inevitably involves almost constantly looking up instructions to find their code numbers.

Assembly language uses a program in the computer to take three or four letter codes and convert these into the corresponding machine code instruction numbers. Most assemblers also provide the programmer with some further assistance, but not much when compared to a high level language such as BASIC. The main function of the assembler is simply to take the three or four letter mnemonics, convert them to the appropriate numbers, and store these in the required area of the computer's memory. An assembler is really the most basic of compilers, but as far as the programmer is concerned there is no real difference between assembly language and machine code, and if you can program in one you can also program using the other.

Of course, the main advantage of using an assembler is that the mnemonics are chosen to closely relate to the instructions that they represent. For example, the Return Form Subroutine instruction has RTS as its mnemonic, which is obviously much easier to remember than the machine code number of 20085. If you intend to do a lot of machine code programming an assembler could reasonably be considered essential, since using anything other than a few short machine code routines is generally rather awkward and inconvenient with a home-computer which was designed primarily for BASIC programming. This is especially the case with a computer such as the Sinclair QL, which has an advanced microprocessor that makes assembly language programming in many ways a relatively simple task, but where machine code programming is a very slow and tedious task indeed. The facilities offered vary somewhat from one assembler to another, but most give at least some aid with debugging, although they are nothing like as sophisticated as the best BASIC languages in this respect. Some simple machine code routines are included in the final section of this book so that you can try out a few programs on the QL, but if you intend to write machine code programs for practical applications it would definitely be advisable to enlist the aid of a good assembler.

One final point to bear in mind is that a high level language such as BASIC varies only slightly from one computer to another, and once you have mastered BASIC it is usually not too difficult to write programs for any computer equipped with some form of this language. Problems can arise with the sound and graphics facilities which vary from one machine to another, giving inevitable variations in the sound and graphics commands, and some versions are more comprehensive than others. However, the language is fundamentally the same for all the computers that use it. Machine code programming is identical for any computers that use the 68008 microprocessor as the central processor. Although there are again differences in the sound and graphics facilities available on various machines, these do not affect the instructions that are available to the programmer (although to produce the desired effect it might be necessary to use a different routine for each machine because of differences in the supporting hardware for the microprocessor). The situation is very different when dealing with a computer that uses a different microprocessor such as the 6502. Apart from the differences in the sound and graphics facilities, the microprocessor will have different machine code numbers for each instruction, and probably even different mnemonics. For instance, the 68008 Return From Subroutine instruction, as mentioned earlier, has RTS as its mnemonic, and 20085 is the instruction number. The equivalents for the popular Z80 microprocessor are RET and 169. Furthermore, the instruction sets of various microprocessors are substantially different, as are the registers they contain and the way in which they handle certain tasks. Obviously all microprocessors work on the same basic principle, but rewriting a machine code program to run on a different microprocessor is not usually just a matter of converting the mnemonics or code numbers, and changing from programming one type to programming an alternative device usually involves a fairly substantial amount of work. In practice this means that you should be able to program any 68008 based computer after conquering machine programming

4

on the QL, but might find it difficult to program other computers using machine code.

The Processor

Although a microprocessor is an extremely complex device, usually containing the equivalent of tens of thousands of components, as far as the programmer is concerned it can be regarded as a fairly simple set of electrical circuits known as registers which will perform certain functions if fed with the appropriate instruction numbers. The registers consist of one or more circuits known as flip/flops, and these can produce an output voltage that is either virtually zero, or one that is typically about 5 volts. From the software point of view the voltages are not important, and we can think in terms of low or logic 0 if the output of a flip/flop is near zero volts, and high or logic 1 if it is at about 5 volts. A circuit with an output that can represent just 0 or 1 may not seem to be very useful, and in isolation such a circuit is not of tremendous value, but as we shall see later, a number of flip/flops together can represent large numbers, and can be used to perform complex calculations etc.

The registers of the 68008 are shown in diagramatic form in Figure 1, and this diagram may be a little meaningless to you at this stage. In fact the register set of the 68008 is a little unusual by conventional standards, and this diagram would probably be meaningless to someone who is only familiar with one of the popular 8 bit microprocessors such as the 6502 or the Z80. Most microprocessors have a register called the accumulator, or in some cases there are two of these registers. The accumulator is an extremely important register since any manipulation of data (addition, subtraction, etc.) normally takes place in this register, or to be more accurate, the result of any data manipulation is placed in this register. The calculations are actually handled by the arithmetic logic unit (ALU), but this is something with which the programmer does not become directly involved. If you give the microprocessor certain instructions it carries them out and performs a given task. Exactly how it manages to do this is something

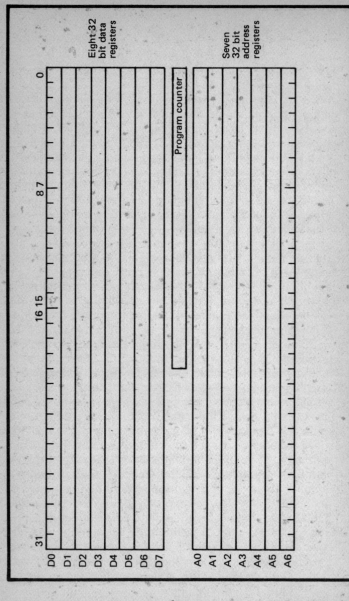

Eight 32 bit data registers

Seven 32 bit address registers

Program counter

0 7 8 15 16 31

D0
D1
D2
D3
D4
D5
D6
D7

A0
A1
A2
A3
A4
A5
A6

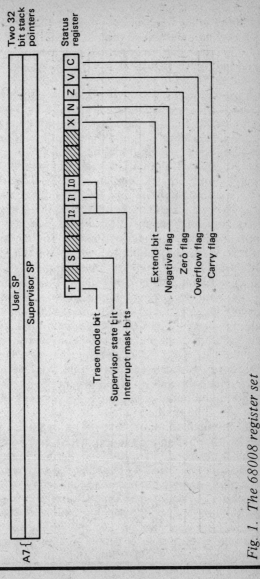

Fig. 1. The 68008 register set

that the programmer does not usually need to understand.

Looking at the register set there is an obvious omission in that there is no accumulator. In fact the 68008 is a highly advanced microprocessor which has the eight data registers instead. These can all operate as accumulators, and can also act as index registers or counters (something we will consider in more detail later).

The seven address registers can be used as index registers, or as straightforward address registers. They are not normally used to hold data. In order to understand the function of the various registers it is really necessary to understand, amongst other things, the basic make-up of a computer. Figure 2 shows in block diagram form the general arrangement used in a 68008 based computer. The memory is a bank of 8 bit registers which are used to store both program instructions and data. The number of registers in the memory block varies from one computer to another, but the 68008 can operate with a maximum of 1048576 (the unexpanded QL actually utilizes only about 25% of the available range). The address bus is 20 bits wide, and these twenty bits are produced by the program counter (see Figure 1). It is the program counter, via the address bus, that selects the particular memory register that is connected to the microprocessor. The data bus is used to transfer data between the microprocessor and the memory block. An important point to note here is that the data bus is bidirectional, and is used by the microprocessor to take data and instructions from memory, and to place data in memory. There are not separate input and output busses on a microprocessor — the data bus is used for both types of operation.

Most microprocessors have 8 bit registers, with some possibly arranged in pairs to effectively form 16 bit registers. Apart from the status register, all the 68008's registers are 32 bits long. This enables large numbers to be handled much more easily and rapidly than is possible using an 8 bit microprocessor, and is certainly a big advantage in many practical applications. Most of the microprocessors in the 68000 range have a 16 bit wide data bus, and therefore have to take in and send out 32 bit chunks of data in two sections to the 16 bit memory registers. The 68008 has only an 8 bit data bus, and

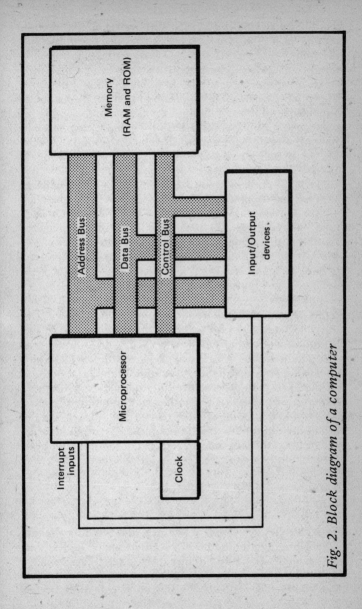

Fig. 2. Block diagram of a computer

therefore has to handle 32 bit chunks of data in four sections (and the memory registers are only 8 bit types). As far as the programmer is concerned this is only of academic importance since the microprocessor automatically takes in or outputs four 8 bit pieces of data, and to a large extent there is no difference between 68000 and 68008 programs. The hardware is obviously different, but this is not of importance to the programmer. The 8 bit data bus of the 68008 does make it somewhat slower in operation than the devices in the 68000 series which have a 16 bit data bus, but this is unlikely to be of any significance in practice.

The 68008 does not have to deal with 32 bit blocks of data, and it can handle data in 8 or 16 bit chunks where this would be more convenient. A collection of 8 bits of data is normally termed a byte, and this is the size in which most microprocessors handle data. Things are different in the case of the 68008 with its 16 and 32 bit capability, and a different terminology is needed. The system that seems to have become established, and the one we will use in this book, is to retain the word byte for 8 bits, and to augment this with *word* for 16 bits of data, and *long word* to cover 32 bits of data. The way in which numbers can be represented by a series of 1s and 0s is something we will consider shortly.

Returning to Figure 2, the control bus is used to make sure that all the elements of the system are operating in unison, and that if (say) the microprocessor sends data to a particular register in memory, that register is ready to receive that data and is not trying to output data to the microprocessor. All the lines in the control bus operate automatically, are not directly controlled by the programmer, and are not something we need concern ourselves with here.

Binary

The 20 bit program counter can place 1048576 different output combinations onto the address bus, and it is this that limits the 68008 to 1048576 memory registers. Each memory register occupies an address, which is merely a number from 0 to 1048575, and each of the output combinations of the program counter corresponds to one of these addresses. Therefore, by placing each bit of the program counter at the appropriate state, the microprocessor can read the contents of any memory register, or can write data to that register, depending on the type of instruction it is executing. In order to undertake machine code or assembly language programming it is essential to understand the way in which the bits of the address bus (and the data bus) are used to represent a number.

The numbering system we normally use is commonly called the decimal system and is, of course, based on the number 10. There are ten single digit numbers from 0 to 9. This system of numbering is not very convenient for an electronic circuit in that it is difficult to devise a practical system where an output has ten different voltage levels so that any single digit decimal number can be represented. It is much easier to use simple flip/flops which have just two output levels, and can only represent 0 or 1. However, this bars such circuits from operating directly in the decimal numbering system. Instead, the binary system of numbering is utilised.

This system is based on the number 2 rather than 10, and the highest single digit number is 1 rather than 9. If we take a decimal number such as 238, the 8 represents eight units (10 to the power of 0), the 3 represents three tens (10 to the power of 1), and the two represents 2 hundreds (10 to the power of 2 or 10 squared). Things are similar with a binary number such as 1101. Working from right to left again, the 1 represents the number of units (2 to the power of 0), the 0 represents the number of twos (2 to the power of 1), the next 1 represents the number of fours (2 to the power of 2), and the final 1 represents the number of eights (2 to the power of 3). 1101 in binary is therefore equivalent to 13 in decimal (1 + 0 + 4 + 8 = 13).

The table given below shows the number represented by each digit of a 16 bit number when it is set high. Of course, a bit always represents zero when it is set low.

Bit	0	1	2	3	4	5	6
	1	2	4	8	16	32	64

Bit	7	8	9	10	11•	12
	|	|	|	|	|	|
	128	256	512	1024	2048	4096

Bit	13	14	15
	|	|	|
	8192	16384	32768

Using 16 bits any integer from 0 to 65535 can be represented in binary fashion, or using 8 bits any integer from 0 to 255 can be represented, and this exposes the main weakness of the binary numbering system. Numbers of modest magnitude are many binary digits in length, but despite this drawback the ease with which electronic circuits can handle binary numbers makes this system the only practical one at the present time. With its 32 bit registers the 68008 can actually handle very large numbers without difficulty (numbers in excess of 1000 million in fact).

Addition of two binary numbers is a straightforward business which is really more simple than decimal addition. A simple example is shown below:—

First number	11110000
Second number	01010101
Answer	101000101

As with decimal addition, start with the units column and gradually work towards the final column on the left. In this case there is 1 and 0 in the units column, giving a total of 1 in the units column of the answer. In the next column two 0s give 0 in the answer, and the next two columns are equally straightforward. In the fifth one there are two 1s to be added, giving a total of 2. Of course, in binary the figure 2 does not exist, and this should really be thought of as 10 (one 2 and no units), and it is treated in the same way as ten in decimal addition. The 0 is placed in the answer and the 1 is carried forward to the next column of figures. The sixth column again gives a total of 10, and again the 0 is placed in the answer and the 1 is carried forward. In the seventh column this gives a total of 3 in the decimal, but in this binary calculation it must be thought of as the binary number 11 (one 2 and one unit). Therefore, 1 is placed in the answer and 1 is carried forward. In the eighth column this gives an answer of 10, and as there are no further columns to be added, both digits are placed in the answer.

Adding two 8 bit binary numbers together produces a slight complication in that, as in this case, the answer is some 9 bits long. When a data register is used to add two numbers it cannot always accommodate the extra bit when there is a final carry-forward, but the 1 in the last column is not simply lost (which would obviously give an incorrect answer and would be unacceptable). Instead, the carry forward is taken to one bit of the microprocessor's status register. Not surprisingly, this is called the carry or C register. Like the other status registers this is used to control conditional instructions (i.e. if the carry bit is set high do this, if it is not do that). Anyone who has done some BASIC programming should be familiar with conditional instructions in the form of BASIC IF . . . THEN or IF . . . THEN . . . ELSE instructions. There are other types of instruction which can produce a carry forward, and these normally activate the carry register (or carry flag as it is often termed) when appropriate.

Signed Binary

The binary system described so far, which is often called direct binary, is inadequate in many practical applications in that it is unable to handle negative numbers. One way around the problem is to use signed binary numbers where the first bit is used to denote whether the number is positive or negative. The convention has the first bit as a 0 for positive numbers and as a 1 for negative numbers. With this system the normal number range of 0 to 255 is replaced with a range of -127 (11111111) to $+127$ (01111111). The problem is solved only at the expense of reduced maximum magnitude for a given number of bits. Note though, that where two or more bytes (or words, or long words) are used to form a long number, only the most significant bit of the high byte needs to be used to indicate whether the number is positive or negative, and it is not necessary to use the most significant bit of each byte in the number to do this.

Obviously a certain amount of care needs to be exercised when dealing with binary numbers and you must know whether a number is in signed or unsigned binary. For example, 10000001 could be 129 (unsigned) or −1 (signed). In this basic form the signed binary system has practical limitations in that it can represent binary numbers without any difficulty, but calculations fail to give the right result, which makes the system of little practical value unless it is modified to correct this anomaly. It is not used with the 68008 microprocessor in the basic form described above.

To illustrate the problem, consider the calculation shown below:−

16	00010000
−5	10000101
Answer (−21)	10010101

Adding 16 and −5 should obviously give an answer of 11 and not −21.

An alternative and related method of handling negative number is the ones complement system. Here a negative number is the complement of the positive equivalent. For instance, +16 in binary is 00010000, and −16 is therefore 11101111. In other words, the ones are simply changed to zeros and the zeros are changed to ones. This gives better results when used in calculations, as demonstrated by the example given below:−

16	00010000
−5	11111010
Answer (266)	100001010

14

This answer may seem to be less use than the one obtained using ordinary signed binary, and the margin of error is certainly greater, but this depends on how the answer is interpretted. The first point to note is that the positive number starts with a zero and the negative number starts with a 1. Provided that sufficient digits are used this will always be the case, and in this respect the system is not much different to ordinary signed binary. The answer is completely wrong of course, but, if the carry is ignored the answer is much closer to the right result. It then becomes 10 rather than 11. So what happens if we try another example and again ignore the carry in the answer?

32	0010000
−4	1111011
Answer (27)	00011011

As before, the answer is wrong, but is one less than the right answer (which is of course 28 in this case).

Twos Complement

Clearly this system can be made to operate properly, and it is just a matter of finding some way of correcting the answer. The standard method used with most microprocessors, including the 68008 is the "twos complement" system. This differs from the ones complement system in that once the compliment of a number has been produced, one is added to it. Therefore, rather than −5 being represented as 11111010, it becomes 11111011. If we now apply this to one of the examples given earlier we obtain the following result.

16	00010000
−5	11111011
Answer (11)	00001011

This time, provided we ignore the carry, we have the correct answer of 11. This is a convenient way of handling subtraction (for the microprocessor anyway) since subtraction can be handled by the same circuit that handles addition. To handle a sum such as 45 − 25 the figure of 25 is converted into (twos complement) −25, and then added to 45. In other words, rather than calculating the sum in the form 45 − 25 the microprocessor calculates it as 45 + (−25), and either way the answer is 20.

The table given below shows some sample numbers in twos complement form, and should help to clarify the system for you. Note that, like ordinary signed binary, the first digit is used to indicate whether the number is positive or negative.

Number	Positive	Negative
0	00000000	00000000
1	00000001	11111111
2	00000010	11111110
3	00000011	11111101
4	00000100	11111100
32	00100000	11100000
126	01111110	10000010
127	01111111	10000001
128	010000000	10000000

Another point to note is that with 8 bit twos complement numbers the range is from +127 to −128.

So far we have only considered calculations where the answer is a positive quantity, but the twos complement system works properly if the answer is negative. The following example demonstrates this point:—

16	00010000
−31	11100001
Answer (−15)	11110001

The system also functions correctly when two negative numbers are added together, as demonstrated by this example:—

−4	11111100
−8	11111000
Answer (−12)	11110100

Overflow Flag

When using the twos complement system there is a slight problem in that a number can be accidentally turned into a negative quantity. The simple calculation shown below demonstrates this point:—

64	01000000
127	01111111
Answer (−65)	10111111

If taken as an ordinary 8 bit direct binary number this does give the right answer, but in the twos complement system the carry forward from bit 6 to bit 7 has changed the sign and magnitude of the number so that an answer of −65 instead of 191 is obtained (we are only dealing with 8 bit numbers here, but the same thing could obviously happen with 16 or 32 bit numbers).

This is termed an overflow, and it is handled by microprocessors such as the 68008 by a flag called (appropriately) the overflow flag. In the diagram of Figure 1 this is given its abbreviated name, the V flag. Like the carry flag, there are special instructions connected with this flag, and these can be used to prevent erroneous results from being produced, or to give warning that an error has occurred. These flags are normally at 0 and are set by an overflow or a carry forward. They are automatically reset by some of the microprocessor's instructions, and this helps to streamline things so that the system operates rapidly and uses as little memory as possible. The 68008 does not have instructions to specifically set or reset flags of the status register.

17

At this stage it is probably best not to go into any more detail about binary calculations and the way they are handled by microprocessors. It is a complicated subject, and it is probably clarified most easily by trying out a few programs which demonstrate the techniques involved. Some practical examples that can be run on the Sinclair QL computer are given later in this book. Even if you can only understand direct binary, provided you also understand the main principles of microprocessors you should be able to run and understand some simple machine code routines.

Binary Coded Decimal

The 68008 can use another form of binary known as binary coded decimal, or BCD. This is perhaps less frequently used than the twos complement binary system described earlier, and it has the disadvantages of being relatively slow and uneconomic on memory. However, it can be used to give a high degree of precision, and it can be advantageous in certain applications. It is certainly worthwhile considering this system briefly here.

With BCD four binary bits (often termed a nibble) are used to represent each decimal digit. The system operates in the manner shown below:—

Decimal Number	Bit Code
0	0000
1	0001
2	0010
3	0011
4	0100
5	0101
6	0110
7	0111
8	1000
9	1001

The binary number is in fact just the normal binary representation of the number concerned, and it is only for numbers of more than 9 that the system is different. The binary codes from 1010 to 1111 are unused, and all two digit decimal numbers require 8 bit binary codes. For instance, the decimal number 64 would be represented by the 8 bit BCD code 01100100. The first four bits (0110) represent the 6, and the second four bits (0100) represent the four. Each byte can therefore represent any two bit number from 0 to 99, which compares to a range of 0 to 255 for a straightforward 8 bit binary number. This helps to contribute to the relative inefficiency of the BCD system. Of course, when a nibble is incremented by 1 from 1001 (9 in decimal) it does not go to 1010 (which is an illegal code in BCD), but cycles back to 0000. A carry forward of 1 should then be taken to the next BCD nibble.

With this system there is no difficulty in handling large numbers, and it is just a matter of using several bytes to accommodate the required number of digits. Negative numbers and decimal points can also be handled with ease by this system, but this requires several additional digits. This information is usually carried in the most significant bits (i.e. at the left hand end of the number). Some microprocessors handle BCD by performing calculations in ordinary binary and then adjusting the result using a special instruction. The 68008 performs calculations directly in BCD.

Hexadecimal

While on the subject of numbering systems it would perhaps be worthwhile dealing with another system which you will inevitably come across quite frequently, and this is the hexadecimal system. There is in fact yet another system known as octal which, as its name suggests, is based on the number 8. Octal seems to have fallen from favour in recent years, and as it is something you are not likely to encounter these days we will not consider this system here.

A problem with binary numbers is that they tend to have many digits with each digit being either 0 or 1, which makes them rather difficult to deal with in many circumstances. For instance, dealing with large addresses or microprocessor instruction codes in their binary form would probably be beyond most peoples' ability. On the other hand, binary numbers give a graphic representation of the state of each bit in the registers of the microprocessor, and this is something that is often important. Decimal numbers are easier to use in that they are much shorter and are in a familiar form. Converting a decimal number into an equivalent binary one is not a very quick and easy process, especially where large numbers are concerned, and this is inconvenient when it is necessary to visualise things on a bit by bit basis.

The hexadecimal system gives the best of both worlds in that it requires just a few digits to represent fairly large numbers, and is in fact slightly better than the decimal system in this respect. On the other hand, it is easy to convert hexadecimal to binary, and it is easy to use when operating at bit level. The hexadecimal system is based on the number 16, and there are sixteen single digit numbers. Obviously the numbers we normally use in the decimal system are inadequate for hexadecimal as there are six too few of them, but this problem is overcome by augmenting them with the first six letters of the alphabet. It is from this that the system derives its name. The table following helps to explain the way in which the hexadecimal system operates.

What makes hexadecimal so convenient is the way in which multidigit numbers can be so easily converted into binary form. The reason for this is that each hexadecimal digit represents four binary bits. Take the hexadecimal A3 in the following table for instance. The digit A represents 1010 in binary, and the digit three converts to 0011. A3 therefore represents 10100011 in binary. You may find that you can memorise the four bit binary number represented by each of the sixteen hexadecimal digits, but a little mental arithmetic is all that is needed to make the conversion if you cannot.

The digits in a hexadecimal number represent, working from right to left, the number of units 16s, 256s, 4096s, 65536s, and 1048576s. You are unlikely to use hexadecimal numbers of more than six digits in length.

Decimal	Hexadecimal	Binary
0	0	0000
1	1	0001
2	2	0010
3	3	0011
4	4	0100
5	5	0101
6	6	0110
7	7	0111
8	8	1000
9	9	1001
10	A	1010
11	B	1011
12	C	1100
13	D	1101
14	E	1110
15	F	1111
16	10	00010000
17	11	00010001
163	A3	10100011

System Operation

If we now return to the block diagrams of Figures 1 and 2, you should begin to get the idea of how data is moved around the system and processed. At switch-on the microprocessor has all the registers set to zero, including the program counter which uses the numbers stored in the bytes at the bottom of the address range to provide the start address of the computers operating system program. This start-up procedure is not normally of interest to the machine code programmer, since few people design their own systems, and it is certainly only of academic interest to the QL machine code programmer. The program you write will normally go into a section of memory occupied by random access memory (RAM). This is memory where the microprocessor can set its contents at any desired 8 bit binary number, and then read back that number at a later time. The contents of RAM can be changed an unlimited number of times, but reading the contents of RAM does not destroy the data there or affect it in any way. However, when the computer is switched off the contents of RAM are lost. Software such as the computer's operating system and BASIC interpretter are usually in read only memory (ROM) which retains its contents after the computer has been switched off (although the BASIC interpretter or other language does actually have to be loaded from tape or disc on a few machines, but not the QL of course). The contents of ROM are fixed, and writing to ROM does not alter its contents. ROM is not an area of memory that is normally used by the programmer, the exception being when there are useful routines there that can be utilized.

The block marked input/output in Figure 2 includes such things as the keyboard and the chip which produces the television picture. The 68008 uses memory mapped input/output. In other words, the microprocessor reads data from or writes data to input/output devices just as if they were RAM, and they are addressed in exactly the same way. This has the advantage of making programming more straightforward in that using a common set of instructions for memory and input/output operations gives fewer instructions to contend with. A minor drawback is that some of the memory address range is occupied by the input/output devices, but this does not normally seriously deplete the maximum amount of memory that can be included. This is especially so in the case of the 68008 with its massive address range of over 1000000. Incidentally, when dealing with memory it is common for the term k to be used, and this refers to a kilo-byte of memory, which is actually 1024 bytes. A term that is often used with the 68000 series and other advanced microprocessors is M , or mega-bytes of memory. This is 1048576 bytes or words of memory, and the 68008 therefore has a 1M address range.

With the aid of the computer's operating system and either the BASIC interpretter or an assembler, the machine code program is placed in a suitable section of memory, and the program is run by directing the microprocessor to the appropriate address using the appropriate instruction. With the QL, machine code is run from Super-BASIC using the CALL instruction which can include data to be placed in some of the microprocessors registers, as well as the start address of the routine. The CALLed machine code program then operates by fetching an instruction from the specified start address of the program, and then shuffling data around its registers and the memory as it goes through the set of instructions. This may seem a rather vague description of things, but if you can grasp the basic concept of instructions and data being taken from memory, or possibly input/output devices, with the data being processed in some way by the microprocessor before being sent back to a memory location or an output device, then you should not find it difficult to understand a few simple machine code programs and then gradually progress to more complex ones. If you cannot see how the system operates overall, individual machine code instructions could, to say the least, be rather difficult to understand, and even simple programs would certainly be impossible to follow.

A simple example of how the system operates should now be quite easy for you to understand. We will assume that the program must take a number from one memory location, then add this to a number taken from a second address, and then finally place the answer at a third address. There is more than one way of going about this, and the differences occur due to the various addressing modes that the 68008 can use. In other words, we can place the numbers at virtually any addresses we like, and by using the appropriate addressing mode (or modes) and instructions the program can be made to obtain the numbers from the correct addresses. Addressing modes is a fairly complex subject which is considered in detail in a later chapter of this book, and it will not be considered in detail here. The simple addition program could run along the following lines:—

Move immediate data to register D0
Add immediate data to register D0
Move immediate data to register A0
Move contents of D0 to address stored in A0
Return from subroutine

The first instruction takes the data in the byte or bytes of memory immediately following the instruction, and moves it to data register 0. This is known as immediate addressing, and is the most simple type. The data following the instruction is the first number in the calculation. The next instruction adds the immediate data (the second number in the calculation) to the contents of data register 0. In other words it adds together the two numbers and leaves the answer in register D0. The next instruction loads register A0 with immediate data, which in this case is the address where the result of the calculation is to be stored. The next instruction moves the contents of register D0 to the address contained in A0. Of course, the number moved to A0 previously was the address where we wish to store the result of the calculation. Finally, the return from subroutine instruction hands control back to the computer's operating system and terminates the program in a way that will not crash the computer. In fact, in the case of the QL computer another move instruction is needed prior to the return from subroutine instruction in order to ensure that the computer functions normally after the machine code program has been completed. Another point to bear in mind is that the A6 register should not be used in your own programs and is effectively reserved for use by the QL's operating system (refer to the description of the CALL instruction in the QL manual).

Something that will probably have become apparent is that it takes a large number of machine code instructions to achieve quite simple tasks. When programming in a language such as BASIC each instruction is converted into a number of machine code instructions by the interpretter. This is one of the factors which makes writing machine code programs a relatively slow affair.

Something that is less apparent is that most instructions have a very large number of variations. The move instruction for example, can move data from practically any desired location to virtually any desired destination with a variety of addressing modes to choose from. It is also necessary to specify whether the data is a byte, word, or long word. When using an assembler things are relatively straightforward, with an instruction such as: MOVE D0,(A0) being used. This simply moves the contents of register D0 to the memory location addressed by register A0. When using machine code it is necessary to work out the state of each bit in the control code, choosing the states that give not just the required instruction but also the appropriate variation, and then convert this binary number into a decimal one that can be entered into the computer. This helps to make machine code programming a very difficult and long process with the 68008 microprocessor, and is the reason that the use of an assembler has to be recommended for anyone interested in writing more than just a few very short routines.

It should perhaps be explained that although the address registers are 32 bit types, 12 bits are unused when they are used to hold 20 bit addresses. It is bits 20 to 31 that are left unused. Similarly, if a data register is used to hold a word, bits 16 to 31 are not used, and bits 8 to 31 are not utilized if a data register is used to hold a byte.

The Stack

There are a couple of registers in the 68008 (and shown in Figure 1) which we have not yet considered, and we will take a look at the function of these now. These are the two stack pointers (address register A7), one of which is used in the user mode while the other is utilized in the supervisor mode. The idea of these two modes is for the supervisor one to be used by the operating system, and the user mode to be used for any other programs. A few of the 68008 instructions are privileged and are only available in the supervisor mode. There are output pins on the microprocessor which indicate its operating mode and can be used to disable hardware in the user mode so as to restrict user access to areas of memory or input/output devices (restrict rather than prevent access since it is normally possible to call operating system routines that make use of the protected memory or other hardware). This is a subject which you do not really need to become deeply involved in at this stage. It is acceptable for the two stack pointers to have the same register number (A7) since only one or the other can be used, depending on which operating mode the microprocessor is set to.

So far we have only considered the reason for having two stack pointers, and not the purpose of these and the stack itself. The purpose of the stack is to act as a convenient place for temporary data storage, and with some microprocessors the stack is an internal part of the microprocessor. This is often termed a hardware stack. This is in many ways the most elegant solution to the problem, and it has the advantage of giving relatively high operating speed. It has the disadvantage of giving only a relatively small number of registers, and does of course add complexity to the microprocessor.

The 68008, in common with most of the general purpose microprocessors, uses the alternative of a software stack. This is just an area of memory which is reserved for use as the stack, and the system must, of course, provide RAM at the relevant range of addresses. The stack pointer points to an address in this block of RAM, and with the 68008 the stack can be any section of memory that provides RAM. The stack uses the last in − first out (or LIFO) system. In other words, each time data is placed onto the stack the stack pointer is incremented by 1, and each time data is taken from the stack the pointer is automatically decremented by 1. This is often looked on as being analogous to a stack of plates, with plates being loaded one on top of the other, building a pile from the bottom upwards, and then removing plates from the top of the pile and working downwards. This analogy does not work too well with the 68008 as its stack pointer counts downwards as the stack is enlarged. However, the last in − first out doctrine still applies. The fact that the stack grows downwards is largely of academic importance anyway, since the stack pointer increments and decrements automatically.

Apart from use as a convenient temporary data store for general purposes, the stack is also used when subroutines and interrupts are implemented. We will not consider these in detail here, but in both cases the microprocessor breaks out of its normal operating routine, and branches off into another routine. With an interrupt the signal to the microprocessor that it must break out of its normal routine is provided by a hardware device via the 68008's three interrupt inputs. A typical application where interrupts are used is the timer that is a feature of many home-computers. Here a counter circuit generates an interrupt (say) every 10 milliseconds, and a software routine is used to increment by one the number stored at a set of memory locations. With suitable manipulation the number in these RAM locations can be converted into suitable data for a minutes and seconds display, or even for a real-time clock of the type available in the QL computer. If the timer is to achieve a reasonable degree of accuracy it is important that the microprocessor carries out the software routine at each request without waiting to complete other tasks first. It is for this type of application that interrupts are ideal.

The problem with the use of interrupts is that the microprocessor has to be able to break back into its main routine again after it has finished the interrupt routine. To facilitate this it is necessary to store on the stack the contents of any registers that are in use at the time the interrupt occurs. After the interrupt has been serviced the data in the stack is returned to the registers from where it was taken so that the program can then continue where it left off. The general situation is the same when a subroutine is called, and a subroutine could be regarded as a sort of software generated interrupt.

When writing programs for home-computers it is unlikely that you will need to deal with interrupts, and they are principally used as part of the computer's operating system and in a few specialised add-on hardware applications. A detailed description of the 68008's sophisticated system of interrupts would certainly be out of place in an introductory book such as this one. However, it is important to realise that interrupts are occurring while machine code programs are running, since in some applications the disruption caused by interrupts can prevent proper operation of the program. This occurs where the timing of the program is critical, and the delays produced by the interrupts prevent the computer from providing some event at strictly regular intervals. When a program of this type is running it is necessary to disable interrupts.

Flags

The 68008 has status flags apart from the carry and overflow ones, and one of these is the zero flag. This is used by conditional instructions which test to see whether or not this bit is set, and as its name suggests, this bit is set when the result of an operation by the arithmetic logic unit has produced zero as the answer.

The negative flag or N bit is equally straightforward, and this bit is set when the result of an operation by the arithmetic logic unit gives a negative result.

There are three interrupt mask bits in the status register, and these are used to determine which devices connected to the interrupt inputs are able to generate interrupts and which are not. As mentioned earlier, there are three interrupt inputs on the 68008, and the idea is for each device connected to these inputs to produce a binary pattern on these inputs. The lower the number, the higher the priority of the interrupting device. Most microprocessors have a system of interrupts that enables devices which must be serviced most urgently to take precedence over less important devices, but the seven tier system of the 68008 is far superior to most other microprocessors. Note that only seven and not eight different levels of interrupt priority are available since there must be an inactive input state.

The number placed in the interrupt mask bits enables devices having an interrupt priority level equal to or less than that number to generate interrupts. For instance, placing 101 (5 in decimal) in the interrupt mask bits enables devices of priority level 5 or less to generate interrupts. Placing all three masking bits at zero therefore disables interrupts.

The S bit of the status register selects the operating mode, and is set at 1 in the supervisor mode and at 0 in the user mode.

The X or extend bit is a form of carry flag which is used in microprecision arithmetic, and this is something which goes beyond the scope of this book.

An advanced feature of the 68008 is trace mode, and the device is forced into this mode by setting the T bit or trace flag to 1. This is again something which goes beyond the scope of this book, but the basic idea of the trace mode is to enable the processor to go through a program one instruction at a time, enabling the contents of the registers to be examined between instructions. This is something which aids the debugging of programs, and which can be achieved with virtually any microprocessor with the aid of a suitable monitor program, but it is something that is more easily implemented with the 68008 and its trace mode.

Chapter 2

ADDRESSING MODES

Addressing is the means by which the processor determines the location of the data, or operand, on which the instruction is to operate. Some instructions (for example, MOVE) require two addresses, the source location and the destination location.

Most instructions can use more than one addressing mode. Where two addresses are required, a different mode of addressing may be used for each.

The MC68008 has 11 addressing modes.

1. Implicit

In fact, these instructions require no operand as such, though they may store or retrieve data from the stacks. Examples are NOP and RESET, which require no operand at all, and RTE, RTS, RTV and the TRAP instructions, which use one or other of the stacks.

Also in this category are those instructions which make implied reference to one of the 68008 registers. These include Branch and Jump instructions (which alter the program counter), and some MOVE instructions which alter specific registers.

In general, instructions which use implicit addressing can *only* use implicit addressing.

2. Register Addressing

This mode is used to specify an operand residing in one of the 68008's internal registers. It is subdivided into two self-explanatory modes, Data Register Direct, and Address Register Direct.

Most 68008 instructions allow Register addressing, but there are a few which can only use registers as operands.

These are EXG (exchange registers), EXT (sign extend), and SWAP (swap register contents). Certain MOVE instructions can also only use registers as operands.

There are also some instructions which require that one of the operands be specifically either an address or a data register. For example, the ADD instruction requires one operand to be a data register, and the ADDA instruction requires one operand to be an address register.

3. Immediate Addressing

In this mode, the data follows immediately after the opcode within the program in memory. This addressing mode is used to include constant data within programs.

The 68008 has instructions for immediate data which can be of byte, word (two byte), or long word (four byte) length. This is indicated by appending B , W , or L to the instruction, for example ADD.L or SUB.B. Word length is assumed if no indication is given.

The 68008 also has a 'quick' immediate addressing mode for small operands. In these, the data is actually contained within the opcode. ADDQ and SUBQ can add and subtract numbers from 1 to 8. MOVEQ can be used to move numbers from 0 to 255 (or −128 to +127) in 2's complement) to a register or memory location.

In assembly language, immediate addressing is indicated by preceding the data with a 'hash' sign (#), thus:—

MOVE #2000,D3

This instruction would load 2000 (decimal) into the register D3.

4. Absolute Short Addressing

Absolute addressing means that the address of the data follows immediately after the opcode in memory.

In absolute short addressing, the low-order half of the address follows directly after the opcode in memory. The high-order half of the address is assumed to be either 0000 or FFFF (hex.), depending on whether bit 15 is 0 or 1. This means if the two bytes following the opcode contain 0000 to 7FFF, this will be the address of the data, but if they contain 8000 to FFFF, the addresses accessed will be from FFFF8000 to FFFFFFFF. Thus this mode can address the top 32K bytes of memory, and the bottom 32K. This is called 'sign extension', because bit 15 would be the sign bit in 2's complement representation.

It should be noted that the 68008 processor used in the Sinclair QL can only address memory locations up to FFFFF hex. Also, the bottom 32K of memory in the QL is occupied by the system ROM.

This mode of addressing will be used automatically by an assembler when appropriate. It saves memory space and time compared to absolute long addressing.

5. Absolute Long Addressing

In this mode, the four bytes after the opcode contain the addressing where the data is to be found. This mode allows the processor to access any byte in memory, though it is not used where absolute short addressing can be used. Again, it must be remembered that the 68008 can only use addresses up to FFFFF hex.

Address Register Indirect Addressing

In indirect addressing, an address in memory follows the opcode, and the contents of this memory location are the address from which the data must be fetched. The 68008 series microprocessors do not provide true indirect addressing (in fact very few processors do), but they do allow the address of the data to be held in one of the processor's address registers.

In assembly language, register indirect mode is indicated by enclosing the address register to be used in brackets, thus:—

MOVE D1,(A5)

This instruction means 'move the contents of register D1 to the memory location addressed by A5'.

6. Address Register Indirect with Displacement

This is similar to address register indirect, but the address in the register is modified by an offset which follows the opcode in program memory, and is therefore normally a constant offset. This mode is useful when we want to access a particular item in an array or list. The base address of the array is contained in the address register, and the various elements can be accessed by the offsets following the instructions.

In assembly language, this mode is indicated by placing the offset before the address register (which is enclosed in brackets, as for register indirect), thus:—

MOVE 40(A5),D0

This instruction means 'move the contents of the memory location in register A5+40 bytes to register D0'.

Note that this mode does not alter the contents of the address register.

7. Address Register Indirect with Index and Displacement

This is a further extension of the preceding mode, the address of the data being the sum of three elements; the contents of an address register, the contents of an index register (which can be any data or address register), and a displacement included in the instruction.

This is used for similar purposes to the preceding mode, but it is more useful for structured data. The address register can contain the base address of the data, the index register can be used to point to a particular record in the data, and the displacement to a particular part of the record.

The assembly language form is a fairly obvious extension of the foregoing modes, with the address register and the index register included together in the brackets, thus:—

$$MOVE\ 40(A0,A1),D0$$

This means 'move the contents of memory location (A0+A1+40) to D0.

8. Address Register Indirect with Postincrement

This mode is used when accessing successive bytes in memory, as for example when printing a string or moving a block of memory, or when accessing successive elements in an array of data.

The address in the base register can be incremented by one, two, or four bytes after each operation, depending on whether the byte, word or long word form of the instruction is in use.

This mode is indicated in assembly language by placing a ' + ' sign after the closing bracket around the address register, thus:—

$$MOVE.B\ (A1)+,D1$$

This instruction means 'load the contents of the memory location addressed by register A1 into register D1, then increment A1 by 1'.

9. Address Register Indirect with Predecrement

This is essentially similar to the foregoing, but is used to move backwards through memory rather than forwards. This may be preferred for some operations, and is essential for moving a block of memory downwards (i.e. to lower addresses) when the new addresses overlap the old.

In this case, the contents of the address register are modified before the operation is carried out rather than after. This order of postincrement but predecrement is used to maintain consistency with the way in which the 68008 stack pointers operate.

This mode is indicated in assembly language by putting a ' — ' sign *before* the brackets enclosing the address register, thus:—

MOVE.L —(A1),D1

This instruction means 'decrement the contents of register A1 by 4 (long word form) then move the contents of the memory location addressed by A1 to register D1'.

10. Program Counter Relative with Displacement

This is really a special case of register indirect addressing, but using the program counter rather than one of the address registers. This means that a program can run correctly wherever it is loaded in memory, because all addresses can be specified relative to the current position in the program. In other words, it is an aid to writing 'position independent code'.

This mode is similar to register indirect with displacement, in that the instruction contains a constant displacement after the opcode.

The assembly language form is also similar, but with 'PC' in place of an address register in the brackets, thus:—

MOVE 20(PC),D2

11. Program Counter Relative with Index and Displacement

This is an extension to the previous mode, and is provided for the same reasons. It is essentially similar to register indirect with index and displacement, but using the program counter in place of an address register.

The index register can be any of the address or data registers.

The allowable assembly language forms for this mode vary somewhat between different assemblers, and it would probably not be helpful to give examples here. The documentation with an assembler should include this information.

Chapter 3

THE INSTRUCTION SET

In this chapter, all the 68008 instructions are described. The address modes available for each instruction are given in chart form, except where only one mode is available (mostly instructions using implied addressing).

Charts of opcodes are not given. The way in which the registers, for instance, are coded within instruction codes, makes the opcodes very tricky to calculate, even for experts. Hand assembling for 68000-series microprocessors is simply not a practical proposition.

Where the result of an operation has to be stored, it is to be assumed that it is stored in the destination data location unless otherwise indicated.

ADD BINARY CODED DECIMAL
Mnemonic — ABCD

This instruction adds the source data and the value of the extend flag X to the destination data, using binary coded decimal (BCD) arithmetic.

This instruction can use either register direct addressing or address register indirect addressing, but both operands must use the same mode. It can therefore be used for register-to-register addition, or memory-to-memory addition. Only the least significant 8 bits of the data are affected.

When address register indirect addressing is used, the addresses in both registers are decremented before the addition. This is to simplify multi-byte BCD arithmetic. Strings of BCD digits are normally stored with the least significant digit at the highest memory address.

The carry (C) and extend (X) flags are set if a decimal carry is generated, and are cleared otherwise. The zero (Z) flag is cleared if the result is non-zero, unchanged otherwise. Note this: the zero flag is not changed if the result is zero. In multiple precision arithmetic, the zero flag should be set first. If any part of the result is non-zero, the flag will be cleared, otherwise it will remain set. The N and V flags are undefined.

ADD BINARY
Mnemonic — ADD

This instruction adds the source data to the destination data, storing the result in the destination. One of the operands for this instruction must be a data register. All address modes except implied can (in general) be used for the other operand, but it must be remembered that address registers cannot handle byte-size data (see charts).

The C and X flags are set if a carry is generated and cleared otherwise. The Z flag is set if the result is zero and cleared otherwise. The N flag is set if the result is negative and cleared otherwise. The V flag is set if an overflow occurs and is cleared otherwise.

Address Mode	Source	Destination
Data register direct	x	x
Address register direct		
Address register indirect		x
Postincrement register indirect		x
Predecrement register indirect		x
Register indirect with offset		x
Register indirect with index		x
Absolute short		x
Absolute long		x
P.C. relative with offset		
P.C. relative with index		
Immediate		

Address Mode	Source	Destination
Data register direct	x	x
Address register direct	x	
Address register indirect	x	
Postincrement register indirect	x	

Address Mode	Source	Destination
Predecrement register indirect	x	
Register indirect with offset	x	
Register indirect with index	x	
Absolute short	x	
Absolute long	x	
P.C. relative with offset	x	
P.C. relative with index	x	
Immediate	x	

ADD ADDRESS
Mnemonic — ADDA

This is a special form of the ADD instruction to allow a source operand to be added to a specific address register. All address modes are allowed for the source operand. Note that this instruction *does not* affect *any* of the status flags.

Address Mode	Source	Destination
Data register direct	x	
Address register direct	x	x
Address register indirect	x	
Postincrement register indirect	x	
Predecrement register indirect	x	
Register indirect with offset	x	
Register indirect with index	x	
Absolute short	x	
Absolute long	x	
P.C. relative with offset	x	
P.C. relative with index	x	
Immediate	x	

ADD IMMEDIATE
Mnemonic - ADDI

This instruction performs decimal addition between immediate data and the source operand.

Address Mode	Source	Destination
Data register direct		x
Address register direct		
Address register indirect		x
Postincrement register indirect		x
Predecrement register indirect		x
Register indirect with offset		x
Register indirect with index		x
Absolute short		x
Absolute long		x
P.C. relative with offset		
P.C. relative with index		
Immediate	x	

The effect on status flags is the same as for ADD.

ADD QUICK
Mnemonic – ADDQ

This is a special form of immediate-addressing addition for small source operands (i.e. 1 to 8). This form has the advantage of being faster and using less memory space.

Address Mode	Source	Destination
Data register direct		x
Address register direct		x
Address register indirect		x
Postincrement register indirect		x
Predecrement register indirect		x
Register indirect with offset		x
Register indirect with index		x
Absolute short		x
Absolute long		x
P.C. relative with offset		
P.C. relative with index		
Immediate	x	

The status flags are affected in the same way as for the ADD instruction.

ADD EXTENDED
Mnemonic — ADDX

Adds the source data plus the value of the X flag to the destination data. As with ABCD, this instruction has register-to-register and memory-to-memory forms. The data size can be byte, word, or long word. It is used in multiple-precision arithmetic.

In the address register indirect (memory to memory) form, the contents of both address registers are automatically decremented before the addition is performed (by 1, 2, or 4 depending on whether the B , W , or L form of the instruction is specified).

The C and X flags are set if a carry is generated, cleared otherwise. The Z flag is clear if the result is non-zero, otherwise unchanged (see ABCD for comment on this). The N flag is set if the result is zero and cleared otherwise. The V flag is set if there is an overflow, cleared otherwise.

LOGICAL AND
Mnemonic — AND

This instruction performs a logical bitwise AND between the source data and the destination data. One of the data registers must be used as either the source or the destination. In general, most other address modes can be used for the other operand, as in the charts.

Address Mode	Source	Destination
Data register direct	x	x
Address register direct		
Address register indirect		x
Postincrement register indirect		x
Predecrement register indirect		x
Register indirect with offset		x
Register indirect with index		x
Absolute short		x
Absolute long		x
P.C. relative with offset		

Address Mode	Source	Destination
P.C. relative with index		
Immediate		

Address Mode	Source	Destination
Data register direct	x	x
Address register direct	x	
Address register indirect	x	
Postincrement register indirect	x	
Predecrement register indirect	x	
Register indirect with offset	x	
Register indirect with index	x	
Absolute short	x	
Absolute long	x	
P.C. relative with offset	x	
P.C. relative with index	x	
Immediate	x	

The N flag will be set if the most significant bit of the result is 1, cleared otherwise. The Z flag will be set if the result is zero, cleared otherwise. The V and C flags are *always* cleared, and the X flag is unaffected.

AND IMMEDIATE
Mnemonic – ANDI

Performs logical bitwise AND between immediate data and the destination operand. The chart shows the available address modes.

Address Mode	Source	Destination
Data register direct		x
Address register direct		x
Address register indirect		x
Postincrement register indirect		x
Predecrement register indirect		x
Register indirect with offset		x
Register indirect with index		x
Absolute short		x

Address Mode	Source	Destination
Absolute long		x
P.C. relative with offset		
P.C. relative with index		
Immediate	x	

In addition, the destination operand may be the condition codes, or the entire status register. If it is the entire status register, this is a privileged instruction and can *only be executed in Supervisor Mode.*

This instruction may be specified as byte, word, or long word. The immediate data supplied must match the operand size specified, that is, one or two words. If a byte operand is specified, the second (low-order) byte is used.

The effect on the status flags is the same as for AND, except, of course, where the status register is the destination. In this case, the flags are set by the result of the operation.

ARITHMETIC SHIFT LEFT (DATA REGISTER)
Mnemonic – ASL

This instruction shifts the contents of a data register to the left. The bit shifted out is placed in the C and X flags, and zeroes are moved in on the right.

Shifting by more than one bit position is allowed. The shift count may be specified by another data register, or immediate data. In the first case, the shift may be from 0 to 63 places, in the latter from 1 to 8.

The C and X flags receive the shifted-out bits. If the shift count is zero, C is cleared and X is unaffected. The V flag indicates any sign change during the operation. The N and Z flags are altered depending on the value of the result.

ARITHMETIC SHIFT LEFT (MEMORY)
Mnemonic – ASL

Similar to the previous instruction, but operates on an operand in memory, is restricted to word-length data, and can shift by one position only.

Address Mode	Source	Destination
Data register direct		
Address register direct		
Address register indirect		x
Postincrement register indirect		x
Predecrement register indirect		x
Register indirect with offset		x
Register indirect with index		x
Absolute short		x
Absolute long		x
P.C. relative with offset		
P.C. relative with index		
Immediate		

The C and X flags are set by bit 15 of the (original) data, the V flag indicates any sign change.

ARITHMETIC SHIFT RIGHT
Mnemonic — ASR

This instruction shifts the bits of the operand to the right. The bits shifted out to the right go into the C and X flags, and zeroes are moved in on the left.

As with ASL, there are versions of this instruction for operations on data registers and memory locations, and the same restrictions and flag indications apply, as do the address modes applicable.

BRANCH ON CONDITION

This group of instructions test the flags, and may cause the program to branch forward or back depending on the results. Thus they are the decision-making instructions.

These instructions are most frequently preceded by a compare instruction, but they may follow any instruction which conditions the flags.

BHI — Branch high
Branches if both the C and Z flags are clear.

BLS — Branch Low or Same
Branches if either the C or Z flag is set.

BCC — Branch if Carry Clear
Self-explanatory.

BCS — Branch if Carry Set
Self-explanatory.

BNE — Branch if Not Equal (to zero)
Branches if the Z flag is clear.

BEQ — Branch if Equal (to zero)
Branches if the Z flag is set.

BVC — Branch if oVerflow Clear
Self-explanatory.

BVS — Branch if oVerflow Set
Self-explanatory.

BPL — Branch if PLus (positive)
Branches if the N flag is clear.

BMI — Branch if MInus (negative)
Branches if the N flag is set.

BGE — Branch if Greater or Equal
Branches if the N and V flags are either both set or both clear.

BLT — Branch if Less Than
Branches if N is set and V is clear, or if N is clear and V is set.

BGT — Branch if Greater Than
Branches if N and V are set and Z is clear, or if N and V and Z are all clear.

BLE – Branch if Less or Equal

Branches if Z is set, or if N is set and V is clear, or if N is clear and V is set.

The only address mode used by these instructions is program counter relative. The displacement from the instruction location can be from −126 to +129, or from −32766 to +32769. Note that these figures represent memory locations, not instructions.

The displacement is added to the program counter after the program counter has been incremented by two.

Branch instructions do not affect the flags. The old value of the program counter is lost.

TEST A BIT AND CHANGE
Mnemonic – BCHG

This instruction tests the state of a bit in a memory location or data register, and complements it. The original state of the bit is reflected in the Z flag. The number of the bit to be tested may be either immediate data, or held in a data register. Allowable address modes for the destination data are shown in the chart.

Address Mode	Source	Destination
Data register direct		x
Address register direct		
Address register indirect		x
Postincrement register indirect		x
Predecrement register indirect		x
Register indirect with offset		x
Register indirect with index		x
Absolute short		x
Absolute long		x
P.C. relative with offset		
P.C. relative with index		
Immediate		

If the bit to be tested is in memory, then BCHG is restricted to byte-size data.

This instruction only affects the Z flag.

TEST A BIT AND CLEAR
Mnemonic — BCLR

This instruction is identical to BCHG, with the exception that the tested bit is always set to zero, regardless of its original condition. For allowable address modes, etc., see BCHG.

Again, only the Z flag is affected.

BRANCH ALWAYS
Mnemonic — BRA

This instruction is in all essentials similar to the conditional branches, except that no testing of flags occurs, and the program always branches. It is thus exactly equivalent to the BASIC GOTO. For information on the range of allowable displacements, etc., see the section on conditional branches.

TEST A BIT AND SET
Mnemonic — BSET

This instruction is identical to BCHG and BCLR, except that the tested bit is always set. See BCGH for allowable address modes, etc.

BRANCH TO SUBROUTINE
Mnemonic — BSR

This instruction is similar to BRA, but before branching it saves the address of the instruction following BSR on the stack. Thus an RTS (return from subroutine) instruction at the end of the subroutine allows program execution to continue with the instruction after BSR.

This instruction allows a relative unconditional jump to a subroutine, and is useful when writing position-independent code.

No flags are affected.

TEST A BIT
Mnemonic — BTST

This belongs to the same family as BCHG, BCLR, and BSET, but in this case, the tested bit is not altered. See BCHG for other information.

CHECK REGISTER AGAINST BOUNDARIES
Mnemonic — CHK

This instruction checks the contents of a data register against a source operand. If the contents of the data register are less than zero or greater than the source operand, a TRAP is generated, and the processor enters exception processing. Only the least significant 16 bits of the data register are used. There are no byte or long word versions of this instruction.

Address Mode	Source	Destination
Data register direct	x	x
Address register direct		
Address register indirect	x	
Postincrement register indirect	x	
Predecrement register indirect	x	
Register indirect with offset	x	
Register indirect with index	x	
Absolute short	x	
Absolute long	x	
P.C. relative with offset	x	
P.C. relative with index	x	
Immediate	x	

This instruction provides a simple means of checking that a block of data has not exceeded the space allowed for it.

The N flag is set if the contents of the data register are less than zero, and cleared if the source data is less than the contents of the data register. The C, V, and Z flags are affected, but are left undefined. The X flag is not affected.

CLEAR AN OPERAND
Mnemonic — CLR

This instruction sets a data register or memory location to zero. The data size for this instruction can be B, W, or L. W is assumed if length is not specified.

Address Mode	Source	Destination
Data register direct		x
Address register direct		
Address register indirect		x
Postincrement register indirect		x
Predecrement register indirect		x
Register indirect with offset		x
Register indirect with index		x
Absolute short		x
Absolute long		x
P.C. relative with offset		
P.C. relative with index		
Immediate		

This instruction always sets the Z flag, and clears the N, V, and C flags. The X flag is not affected.

COMPARE
Mnemonic — CMP

This instruction subtracts the contents of a memory location or data register from the contents of a data register. The result of the subtraction is not stored, but the status flags are set according to the results. Both operands are unchanged.

Address Mode	Source	Destination
Data register direct	x	x
Address register direct	x	
Address register indirect	x	
Postincrement register indirect	x	
Predecrement register indirect	x	
Register indirect with offset	x	
Register indirect with index	x	
Absolute short	x	
Absolute long	x	
P.C. relative with offset	x	
P.C. relative with index	x	
Immediate	x	

Note that address register direct addressing cannot be used if the data size is byte.

The C , N , V , and Z flags are all affected by this operation, the C flag representing a borrow. X is not affected.

Compare instructions are normally followed by a conditional branch.

COMPARE ADDRESS
Mnemonic – CMPA

This is a special version of the CMP instruction using an address rather than a data register as destination operand. Apart from this, and the fact that it can only use word and long-word size operands, it is equivalent to CMP.

Address Mode	Source	Destination
Data register direct	x	
Address register direct	x	x
Address register indirect	x	
Postincrement register indirect	x	
Predecrement register indirect	x	
Register indirect with offset	x	
Register indirect with index	x	
Absolute short	x	

Address Mode	Source	Destination
Absolute long	x	
P.C. relative with offset	x	
P.C. relative with index	x	
Immediate	x	

For the effect on flags, see CMP.

COMPARE IMMEDIATE
Mnemonic — CMPI

This instruction subtracts the immediate data following the opcode from the destination data. The result is discarded, but the status flags are set according to the result of the subtraction. The destination data is unaltered.

This instruction can be specified as B , W , or L size, and the immediate data supplied must match the size specified. If a byte operand is specified, the low-order (second) byte of the immediate data is used.

Address Mode	Source	Destination
Data register direct		x
Address register direct		
Address register indirect		x
Postincrement register indirect		x
Predecrement register indirect		x
Register indirect with offset		x
Register indirect with index		x
Absolute short		x
Absolute long		x
P.C. relative with offset		
P.C. relative with index		
Immediate	x	

For the effect on the status flags, see CMP.

COMPARE MEMORY
Mnemonic — CMPM

This instruction compares the contents of two memory locations, the addresses of which are held in two address registers. This instruction can only use postincrement register indirect addressing. As with other compare instructions, the contents of the memory locations are not altered, but the status flags are modified.

This instruction is useful for searching a block of memory for occurrences of a particular value, starting at the lowest address and continuing to the highest, branching every time an occurrence is found.

The effect on the status flags is the same as for CMP.

TEST CONDITION, DECREMENT, AND BRANCH

This group of instructions are conditional branches which test both the status flags and a data register.

The status flags are tested first. If the condition is met, the next instruction in sequence is executed. If it is not met, the data register contents is decremented by 1. Then the contents of the data register are tested. If it contains −1, the next instruction in sequence is executed. If not, the program branches.

A 16-bit displacement is specified, so the program can branch by from −32766 to +32769 bytes (not instructions).

DBT — True
Branches if true (1).

DBF — False
Branches if false (0).

DBHI — High
Branches if both the C and Z flages are clear.

DBLS — Low or Same
Branches if either the C or Z flag is set.

DBCC – Carry Clear
Self-explanatory.

DBCS – Carry Set
Self-explanatory.

DBNE – Not Equal (to zero)
Branches if the Z flag is clear.

DBEQ – Equal (to zero)
Branches if the Z flag is set.

DBVC – oVerflow Clear
Self-explanatory.

DBVS – oVerflow Set
Self-explanatory.

DBPL – PLus (positive)
Branches if the N flag is clear.

DBMI – MInus (negative)
Branches if the N flag is set.

DBGE – Greater or Equal
Branches if the N and V flags are either both set or both clear.

DBLT – Less Than
Branches if N is set and V is clear, or if N is clear and V is set.

DBGT – Greater Than
Branches if N and V are set and Z is clear, or if N and V and Z are all clear.

DBLE – Less or Equal
Branches if Z is set, or if N is set and V is clear, or if N is clear and V is set.

This instruction is very valuable in implementing repetitive loops, using a data register as a loop counter, as the instruction both tests a condition and decrements the loop count.

This instruction does not affect the status flags.

DIVISION (SIGNED)
Mnemonic — DIVS

This instruction divides the 32-bit contents of a data register (destination operand) by a 16-bit source operand. The division is performed using 2's complement binary arithmetic. A 32-bit result is obtained, consisting of the quotient in the least 16 bits of the destination data register, and the remainder in the most significant 16 bits. The sign of the remainder and the sign of the dividend unless the remainder is zero.

Address Mode	Source	Destination
Data register direct	x	x
Address register direct		
Address register indirect	x	
Postincrement register indirect	x	
Predecrement register indirect	x	
Register indirect with offset	x	
Register indirect with index	x	
Absolute short	x	
Absolute long	x	
P.C. relative with offset	x	
P.C. relative with index	x	
Immediate	x	

The C flag is always cleared. The N flag is set if the quotient is negative and cleared otherwise, but undefined if an overflow occurs. The V flag is set if the source operand is larger than the destination operand (an overflow), and the division is aborted, leaving the operands unchanged. The extend flag X is not affected. The Z flag is set if the quotient is zero, cleared otherwise.

If division by zero (a mathematical paradox) is attempted, the instruction is aborted, and a TRAP is generated. The processor will automatically enter exception processing.

DIVISION (UNSIGNED)
Mnemonic — DIVU

This instruction divides the 32-bit contents of a data register (destination operand) by a 16-bit source operand. The division is performed using unsigned binary arithmetic. A 32-bit result is obtained, consisting of the quotient in the least significant 16 bits, and the remainder in the most significant 16 bits.

Address Mode	Source	Destination
Data register direct	x	x
Address register direct		
Address register indirect	x	
Postincrement register indirect	x	
Predecrement register indirect	x	
Register indirect with offset	x	
Register indirect with index	x	
Absolute short	x	
Absolute long	x	
P.C. relative with offset	x	
P.C. relative with index	x	
Immediate	x	

Apart from the N flag, the flags are set as for the DIVS instruction. The N flag is set if the most significant bit of the quotient is set, cleared otherwise. If an overflow occurs, the N flag is undefined.

The effect of an attempted division by zero is the same as with the DIVS instruction.

LOGICAL EXCLUSIVE-OR
Mnemonic — EOR

This instruction performs a bitwise exclusive-OR of the contents of a data register with the contents of the destination operand.

EOR is performed according to the following rules:—

$$1 \text{ EOR } 1 = 0$$
$$1 \text{ EOR } 0 = 1$$
$$0 \text{ EOR } 0 = 0$$

Address Mode	Source	Destination
Data register direct	x	x
Address register direct		
Address register indirect		x
Postincrement register indirect		x
Predecrement register indirect		x
Register indirect with offset		x
Register indirect with index		x
Absolute short		x
Absolute long		x
P.C. relative with offset		
P.C. relative with index		
Immediate		

The N flag is set if the M.S.B. of the result is set. The Z flag is set if the result is zero, cleared otherwise. V and C are always cleared, and X is not affected.

EXCLUSIVE OR IMMEDIATE
Mnemonic – EORI

Performs the EOR operation between immediate data and the destination operand. See EOR for logic rules.

Address Mode	Source	Destination
Data register direct		x
Address register direct		
Address register indirect		x
Postincrement register indirect		x
Predecrement register indirect		x
Register indirect with offset		x
Register indirect with index		x
Absolute short		x
Absolute long		x

Address Mode	Source	Destination
P.C. relative with offset		
P.C. relative with index		
Immediate	x	

In addition, the destination operand may be the condition codes or the entire status register. When it is the entire status register, the instruction is *Privileged*, and may only be executed while the processor is in supervisor mode.

The effect on the flags is the same as EOR.

EXCHANGE REGISTERS
Mnemonic – EXG

This instruction swaps over the contents of two 32-bit registers. Only register direct addressing is appropriate.

Address Mode	Source	Destination
Data register direct	x	x
Address register direct	x	x
Address register indirect		
Postincrement register indirect		
Predecrement register indirect		
Register indirect with offset		
Register indirect with index		
Absolute short		
Absolute long		
P.C. relative with offset		
P.C. relative with index		
Immediate		

Note that the order in which the registers are given is immaterial – EXG A4,A6 is the same as EXG A6,A4.

The status flags are not affected.

SIGN EXTEND
Mnemonic — EXT

This instruction extends bit 7 (word-length instruction) through bits 8–15, or bit 15 (long-word instruction) through bits 16–31 of a data register.

Only data register direct addressing is appropriate.

The N flag is set if the result is negative, cleared otherwise. The Z flag is set if the result is zero, cleared otherwise. C and V are always cleared, and X is unaffected.

JUMP
Mnemonic — JMP

This instruction loads a new address into the program counter, causing an unconditional jump to that address. The old address is lost.

Address Mode	Source	Destination
Data register direct		
Address register direct		
Address register indirect		x
Postincrement register indirect		
Predecrement register indirect		
Register indirect with offset		x
Register indirect with index		x
Absolute short		x
Absolute long		x
P.C. relative with offset		x
P.C. relative with index		x
Immediate		

No flags are affected.

JUMP TO SUBROUTINE
Mnemonic — JSR

This instruction causes an unconditional jump to a new address, but saves the old address on the stack. This instruction is similar to BSR but uses an absolute address rather than a relative displacement.

Address Mode	Source	Destination
Data register direct		
Address register direct		
Address register indirect		x
Postincrement register indirect		
Predecrement register indirect		
Register indirect with offset		x
Register indirect with index		x
Absolute short		x
Absolute long		x
P.C. relative with offset		x
P.C. relative with index		x
Immediate		

No flags are affected.

LOAD EFFECTIVE ADDRESS
Mnemonic — LEA

This instruction calculates an effective address, and stores it in one of the address registers.

Address Mode	Source	Destination
Data register direct		
Address register direct		x
Address register indirect	x	
Postincrement register indirect		
Predecrement register indirect	x	
Register indirect with offset	x	
Register indirect with index	x	
Absolute short	x	
Absolute long	x	
P.C. relative with offset	x	
P.C. relative with index	x	
Immediate		

No flags are affected.

58

LINK AND ALLOCATE
Mnemonic — LINK

This instruction saves the contents of a specified address register on the stack, and then stores the (updated) stack pointer in that register. A sign-extended 2's complement displacement from the instruction is then added to the stack pointer.

The purpose of this instruction is to allow space (called a 'frame') to be reserved on the stack for local variables in a subroutine. The UNLINK instruction is used at the end of the subroutine to clear up the stack.

Note that the displacement must be a negative number to reserve space. A positive displacement will cause the stack to be overwritten.

No flags are affected.

LOGICAL SHIFT LEFT (DATA REGISTER)
Mnemonic — LSL

This instruction has the same effect as ASL (data register). See that instruction for details.

LOGICAL SHIFT LEFT (MEMORY)
Mnemonic — LSL

This instruction has the same effect as ASL (memory). See that instruction for details.

LOGICAL SHIFT RIGHT
Mnemonic — LSR

This instruction is identical to ASR, except that zeroes are moved into the most significant bit position, instead of it being kept intact.

Address Mode	Source	Destination
Data register direct		
Address register direct		
Address register indirect		x
Postincrement register indirect		x
Predecrement register indirect		x
Register indirect with offset		x
Register indirect with index		x
Absolute short		x
Absolute long		x
P.C. relative with offset		
P.C. relative with index		
Immediate		

Consult the ASR instruction for details of LSR.

The effect on the flags is the same as for ASR, except that the N flag is always cleared (because the MSB is always cleared).

MOVE DATA
Mnemonic — MOVE

This instruction is used to move data. There are very few restrictions on address modes with this instruction. It is the equivalent of the LOAD and STORE instructions provided on other processors, but data can be moved from memory to memory without intermediate use of a processor register.

Address Mode	Source	Destination
Data register direct	x	x
Address register direct	x	
Address register indirect	x	x
Postincrement register indirect	x	x
Predecrement register indirect	x	x
Register indirect with offset	x	x
Register indirect with index	x	x
Absolute short	x	x
Absolute long	x	x
P.C. relative with offset		
P.C. relative with index		
Immediate	x	

Address register direct mode is not valid if the data size is byte.

The data is examined as it is moved, and the N and Z flags are conditioned accordingly. C and V are always cleared, and X is not affected.

MOVE TO CONDITION CODES
Mnemonic — MOVE to CCR

This is a special MOVE instruction which moves the contents of the source byte into the condition code register.

Address Mode	Source	Destination
Data register direct	x	
Address register direct		
Address register indirect	x	
Postincrement register indirect	x	
Predecrement register indirect	x	
Register indirect with offset	x	
Register indirect with index	x	
Absolute short	x	
Absolute long	x	
P.C. relative with offset	x	
P.C. relative with index	x	
Immediate	x	

Clearly, all the flags are affected by this operation.

MOVE TO THE STATUS REGISTER
Mnemonic — MOVE to SR

This is a special MOVE instruction which moves the contents of the source operand into the status register. This is a *Privileged Instruction* and can only be executed in supervisor mode.

Address Mode	Source	Destination
Data register direct	x	
Address register direct		

Address Mode	Source	Destination
Address register indirect	x	
Postincrement register indirect	x	
Predecrement register indirect	x	
Register indirect with offset	x	
Register indirect with index	x	
Absolute short	x	
Absolute long	x	
P.C. relative with offset	x	
P.C. relative with index	x	
Immediate	x	

Clearly, this instruction will affect all bits in the status register.

MOVE FROM THE STATUS REGISTER
Mnemonic — MOVE from SR

This instruction simply stores the 16-bit status register in a specified destination operand. It is not a privileged instruction.

Address Mode	Source	Destination
Data register direct		x
Address register direct		
Address register indirect		x
Postincrement register indirect		x
Predecrement register indirect		x
Register indirect with offset		x
Register indirect with index		x
Absolute short		x
Absolute long		x
P.C. relative with offset		
P.C. relative with index		
Immediate		

No flags (or other bits in the status register) are affected.

62

MOVE USER STACK POINTER
Mnemonic – MOVE USP

This instruction moves the contents of the user stack pointer (A7) to or from a specified address register. It is a *Privileged Instruction* and can only be executed in supervisor mode.

MOVE ADDRESS
Mnemonic – MOVEA

This special MOVE instruction moves the contents of the source operand to a specified address register.

Address Mode	Source	Destination
Data register direct	x	
Address register direct	x	x
Address register indirect	x	
Postincrement register indirect	x	
Predecrement register indirect	x	
Register indirect with offset	x	
Register indirect with index	x	
Absolute short	x	
Absolute long	x	
P.C. relative with offset	x	
P.C. relative with index	x	
Immediate	x	

Only word and long-word operands may be specified. Word operands are sign-extended before being moved to the address register.

This instruction does not affect the flags register.

MOVE MULTIPLE REGISTERS FROM MEMORY
Mnemonic – MOVEM

This instruction causes specified registers to be loaded from consecutive memory locations beginning at the specified effective address.

The registers are loaded in the order D0 through D7, then A0 through A7. The lowest register specified is loaded from the specified effective address.

Address Mode	Source	Destination
Data register direct		
Address register direct		
Address register indirect	x	
Postincrement register indirect	x	
Predecrement register indirect		
Register indirect with offset	x	
Register indirect with index	x	
Absolute short	x	
Absolute long	x	
P.C. relative with offset	x	
P.C. relative with index	x	
Immediate		

In assembly language, the registers to be loaded are separated by the backslash character, thus: D1/D3/D5/A0/A2. Alternatively, a range of consecutive registers may be specified using the minus sign, thus: D0 − D5 (loads D1,D2,D3,D4,D5).

If word-size data is specified, the operands will be sign-extended before being loaded into the registers.

This instruction is used to quickly restore the status of the processor.

No flags are affected.

MOVE MULTIPLE REGISTERS TO MEMORY
Mnemonic − MOVEM

This is the complement of the previous instruction, and is used to store the processor contents quickly in memory.

Address Mode	Source	Destination
Data register direct		
Address register direct		
Address register indirect		x
Postincrement register indirect		

Address Mode	Source	Destination
Predecrement register indirect	x	
Register indirect with offset	x	
Register indirect with index	x	
Absolute short	x	
Absolute long	x	
P.C. relative with offset		
P.C. relative with index		
Immediate		

No flags are affected by this instruction.

MOVE PERIPHERAL DATA
Mnemonic — MOVEP

This instruction causes two or four bytes of data to be transferred between a specified data register and alternate-byte
memory locations. This instruction is intended to simplify
data transfer between the processor and 8-bit peripheral
devices.

The only address mode allowed is address register indirect
with displacement.

The high-order byte of the data register is transferred first,
the low-order byte last. The address register is incremented by
two as each byte is transferred.

No flags are affected.

MOVE QUICK
Mnemonic — MOVEQ

This instruction is a memory and speed-efficient immediate
addressing move instruction for small operands (8-bit). The
data can only be moved to a data register. It is sign-extended
to 32 bits before being stored.

The N flag is set if the data is negative, the Z flag is set
if it is zero. C and V are always cleared. X is not affected.

SIGNED MULTIPLY
Mnemonic — MULS

This instruction multiplies together two 16-bit operands, yielding a 32-bit result, using 2's complement signed binary arithmetic.

Address Mode	Source	Destination
Data register direct	x	x
Address register direct		
Address register indirect	x	
Postincrement register indirect	x	
Predecrement register indirect	x	
Register indirect with offset	x	
Register indirect with index	x	
Absolute short	x	
Absolute long	x	
P.C. relative with offset	x	
P.C. relative with index	x	
Immediate	x	

The low-order word of the data register is the operand used in the multiplication. The high-order half is ignored, and is overwritten by the result.

N is set if the result is negative, cleared otherwise. Z is set if the result is zero, cleared otherwise. C and V are always cleared, X is not affected.

UNSIGNED MULTIPLY
Mnemonic — MULU

This instruction multiplies together two 16-bit operands, yielding a 32-bit result, using unsigned binary arithmetic.

Address Mode	Source	Destination
Data register direct	x	x
Address register direct		
Address register indirect	x	
Postincrement register indirect	x	

Address Mode	Source	Destination
Predecrement register indirect	x	
Register indirect with offset	x	
Register indirect with index	x	
Absolute short	x	
Absolute long	x	
P.C. relative with offset	x	
P.C. relative with index	x	
Immediate	x	

The low-order word of the data register provides the operand. The high-order word is ignored, and is overwritten by the result.

N is set if the MSB of the result is set, cleared otherwise. Z is set if the result is zero, cleared otherwise. C and V are always cleared, and X is not affected.

NEGATE DECIMAL WITH EXTEND
Mnemonic — NBCD

This instruction subtracts the destination operand and the value of the X flag from zero, and stores the result in the destination. BCD arithmetic is used.

Address Mode	Source	Destination
Data register direct		x
Address register direct		
Address register indirect		x
Postincrement register indirect		x
Predecrement register indirect		x
Register indirect with offset		x
Register indirect with index		x
Absolute short		x
Absolute long		x
P.C. relative with offset		
P.C. relative with index		
Immediate		

This instruction always operates on only one byte of data.

The C and X flags are set if a borrow occurred, cleared otherwise. The Z flag is cleared if the result is non-zero, unaltered if it is zero. The N and V flags are undefined. See ABCD for a comment on the Z flag.

NEGATE
Mnemonic — NEG

This instruction subtracts the destination operand from zero using 2's complement binary arithmetic, storing the result in the destination.

Address Mode	Source	Destination
Data register direct		x
Address register direct		
Address register indirect		x
Postincrement register indirect		x
Predecrement register indirect		x
Register indirect with offset		x
Register indirect with index		x
Absolute short		x
Absolute long		x
P.C. relative with offset		
P.C. relative with index		
Immediate		

C and X are set if a borrow occurs, cleared otherwise. N is set if the result is negative, cleared otherwise. The V flag is set if an overflow occurs, cleared otherwise.

NEGATE WITH EXTEND
Mnemonic — NEGX

This instruction subtracts the destination operand and the value of the X flag from zero, storing the result in the destination.

Address Mode	Source	Destination
Data register direct	x	
Address register direct		
Address register indirect	x	
Postincrement register indirect	x	
Predecrement register indirect	x	
Register indirect with offset	x	
Register indirect with index	x	
Absolute short	x	
Absolute long	x	
P.C. relative with offset		
P.C. relative with index		
Immediate		

This instruction is similar to NEG, but is for use in multiple-precision arithmetic.

C and X are set if a borrow occurs, cleared otherwise. The N flag is set if the result is negative, cleared otherwise. The Z flag is cleared if the result is non-zero, unchanged if it is zero. The V flag is set if there is an overflow, cleared otherwise. For a comment on the Z flag, see ABCD.

NO OPERATION
Mnemonic – NOP

Does nothing except advance the program counter. It can be used to replace instructions that are no longer needed, without having to recompute displacements, to produce a precise time delay, or to temporarily replace instructions you do not want to execute when debugging. It is rarely found in finished programs.

LOGICAL NOT (COMPLEMENT)
Mnemonic – NOT

This instruction performs a bitwise complement of the destination operand. All 0's are changed to 1's and all 1's to 0's, i.e. it is a 1's complement operation.

Address Mode	Source	Destination
Data register direct		X
Address register direct		
Address register indirect	X	
Postincrement register indirect		X
Predecrement register indirect		X
Register indirect with offset		X
Register indirect with index		X
Absolute short		X
Absolute long		X
P.C. relative with offset		
P.C. relative with index		
Immediate		

N is set if the result is negative, cleared otherwise. Z is set if the result is zero, cleared otherwise. C and V are always cleared, and X is unaffected.

LOGICAL INCLUSIVE-OR
Mnemonic — OR

This instruction performs the inclusive-OR operation between the source data and the destination data.

Inclusive-OR is performed according to the following rules:

$$1 \text{ OR } 1 = 1$$

$$1 \text{ OR } 0 = 1$$

$$0 \text{ OR } 0 = 0$$

There are two general forms, depending whether a data register provides the source or the destination operand.

Address Mode	Source	Destination
Data register direct	X	X
Address register direct		
Address register indirect	X	
Postincrement register indirect	X	
Predecrement register indirect	X	

70

Address Mode	Source	Destination
Register indirect with offset	x	
Register indirect with index	x	
Absolute short	x	
Absolute long	x	
P.C. relative with offset	x	
P.C. relative with index	x	
Immediate	x	

Address Mode	Source	Destination
Data register direct	x	x
Address register direct		
Address register indirect		x
Postincrement register indirect		x
Predecrement register indirect		x
Register indirect with offset		x
Register indirect with index		x
Absolute short		x
Absolute long		x
P.C. relative with offset		
P.C. relative with index		
Immediate		

N is set if the result is negative, cleared otherwise. Z is set if the result is zero, cleared otherwise. C and V are always cleared, and X is not affected.

INCLUSIVE-OR IMMEDIATE
Mnemonic — ORI

Performs the inclusive-OR operation between immediate data and the destination operand.

Address Mode	Source	Destination
Data register direct		x
Address register direct		
Address register indirect		x
Postincrement register indirect		x
Predecrement register indirect		x

Address Mode	Source	Destination
Register indirect with offset		x
Register indirect with index		x
Absolute short		x
Absolute long		x
P.C. relative with offset		
P.C. relative with index		
Immediate	x	

In addition, the destination may be the condition codes or the entire status register. If it is the entire status register, this is a *Privileged Instruction*, and can only be executed in supervisor mode.

The data size may be byte, word or long-word. The immediate data supplied must match the operation size. If byte-size data is specified, the low-order (second) byte of the immediate data word is used.

The effect on the flags is the same as for OR.

PUSH EFFECTIVE ADDRESS
Mnemonic – PEA

This instruction calculates an address using one of the control addressing modes, then pushes that address on the stack.

Address Mode	Source	Destination
Data register direct		
Address register direct		
Address register indirect	x	
Postincrement register indirect		
Predecrement register indirect		
Register indirect with offset	x	
Register indirect with index	x	
Absolute short	x	
Absolute long	x	
P.C. relative with offset		
P.C. relative with index		
Immediate		

No flags are affected.

RESET EXTERNAL DEVICES
Mnemonic – RESET

This instruction simply causes a pulse on the RESET pin of the processor, as a reset signal to external devices. The only effect within the processor is to increment the program counter by 2. There is no change to other registers or memory.

ROTATE DATA REGISTER LEFT
Mnemonic – ROL

This instruction rotates the contents of a data register to the left by a number of bit positions which may be contained in another data register, or be given as immediate data. In the first case, rotations of from 0 to 63 bit positions are possible, in the latter from 1 to 8.

The bit shifted out on the left is placed in the carry flag, and it is also moved in to the rightmost bit position.

C is set according to the last bit shifted out to the left. N is set if the MSB is set, cleared otherwise. V is always cleared. Z is set if the result is zero, cleared otherwise.

ROTATE MEMORY WORD LEFT
Mnemonic – ROL

Similar to the preceding instruction, but works on a memory location. The data size is limited to word, and only rotations of one bit position are possible.

Address Mode	Source	Destination
Data register direct		
Address register direct		
Address register indirect		x
Postincrement register indirect		x
Predecrement register indirect		x
Register indirect with offset		x
Register indirect with index		x
Absolute short		x

Address Mode	Source	Destination
Absolute long		x
P.C. relative with offset		
P.C. relative with index		
Immediate		

For the effect on flags, see previous instruction.

ROTATE RIGHT (DATA REGISTER)
Mnemonic – ROR

This instruction rotates the contents of a data register to the right by a number of bit positions, counted as for ROL.

The bit rotated out on the right is placed in the carry flag, and also in the leftmost bit position.

For the effect on the flags, see ROL.

ROTATE RIGHT (MEMORY)
Mnemonic – ROR

Similar to ROR (data register) but works on one word of memory, and rotations are limited to one bit position, as for ROL memory.

Address Mode	Source	Destination
Data register direct		
Address register direct		
Address register indirect		x
Postincrement register indirect		x
Predecrement register indirect		x
Register indirect with offset		x
Register indirect with index		x
Absolute short		x
Absolute long		x
P.C. relative with offset		
P.C. relative with index		
Immediate		

For the effect on flags, see ROL.

74

ROTATE LEFT WITH EXTEND
Mnemonic — ROXL

This instruction is the same as the ROL (register and memory) instructions, except that the leftmost rotated-out bits are echoed in the X flag as well as in C and the rightmost bit position. This version is intended for use in multiple-precision arithmetic.

For details of address modes, etc., see ROL (data register) and ROL (memory word).

ROTATE RIGHT WITH EXTEND
Mnemonic — ROXR

This instruction is the same as the ROR (register and memory) instructions, except that the rightmost shifted-out bits are echoed in the X flag as well as in the C flag and the leftmost bit position. This version is intended for use in multiple-precision arithmetic.

For details of address modes, etc., see ROR (data register) and ROR (memory word).

RETURN FROM EXCEPTION
Mnemonic — RTE

This instruction terminates an exception processing routine, and restores the state of the program by loading the status register, and then the program counter, from the system stack.

After the RTE instruction, the processor may be in user or supervisor mode, depending on the condition of the S bit loaded into the status register.

Obviously, all flags are affected by this instruction.

RETURN AND RESTORE CONDITION CODES
Mnemonic — RTR

This instruction is used to terminate a subroutine. It pulls a word from the stack, and places the 5 least significant bits in the status register. Then it pulls a return address from the stack and loads it into the program counter, thus returning control to the calling program.

There is no instruction that automatically saves the condition codes on the stack when calling a subroutine. To use RTR, you must save the condition codes on the stack at the beginning of the subroutine.

Obviously, all flags may be affected by this instruction.

RETURN FROM SUBROUTINE
Mnemonic — RTS

This instruction is used to terminate a subroutine. It causes control to be returned to the calling program by pulling the return address from the stack and loading it into the program counter.

No flags are affected by RTS, thus with this return instruction the condition codes can be used to pass information from the subroutine to the calling program.

SUBTRACT DECIMAL WITH EXTEND
Mnemonic — SBCD

This instruction subtracts the source data and the value of the X flag from the destination data, using BCD arithmetic.

This instruction can use either register direct addressing, or address register indirect addressing, but both operands must use the same mode. It can therefore be used for register-from-register subtraction, or memory-from-memory subtraction. Only the least significant 8 bits of the data are affected.

The C and X flags are set if a borrow is generated, cleared otherwise. The Z flag is cleared if the result is non-zero, unchanged otherwise (see ABCD for a comment on this). N and V are undefined.

SET ACCORDING TO CONDITION

This instruction tests a specified condition code, and if the condition is met, the contents of a (byte-size) destination operand are set to all ones. If not met, the byte is set to all zeroes.

Address Mode	Source	Destination
Data register direct		x
Address register direct		
Address register indirect		x
Postincrement register indirect		x
Predecrement register indirect		x
Register indirect with offset		x
Register indirect with index		x
Absolute short		x
Absolute long		x
P.C. relative with offset		
P.C. relative with index		
Immediate		

The following is a list of mnemonics and conditions. For an explanation of these conditions see Test Condition, Decrement and Branch.

ST	–	Set True
SF –	–	Set False
SHI	–	Set HIgh
SLS	–	Set Low or Same
SCC	–	Set Carry Clear
SCS	–	Set Carry Set
SNE	–	Set Not Equal
SEQ	–	Set Equal
SVC	–	Set oVerflow Clear
SVS	–	Set oVerflow Set
SPL	–	Set PLus
SMI	–	Set MInus
SGE	–	Set Greater or Equal
SLT	–	Set Less Than
SGT	–	Set Greater Than
SLE	–	Set Less or Equal

No flags are affected by this instruction.

LOAD STATUS REGISTER AND STOP
Mnemonic – STOP

This instruction loads the status register from 16-bit immediate data, and then stops program execution until a trace, interrupt or reset occurs. The program counter is advanced by four to point to the next instruction.

This is a *Privileged Instruction* and can only be executed while in supervisor mode.

SUBTRACT BINARY
Mnemonic – SUB

This instruction subtracts the source operand from the destination operand using binary arithmetic.

There are two general forms of this instruction, with a data register as either the source or the destination operand.

Address Mode	Source	Destination
Data register direct	x	x
Address register direct	x	x
Address register indirect	x	
Postincrement register indirect	x	
Predecrement register indirect	x	
Register indirect with offset	x	
Register indirect with index	x	
Absolute short	x	
Absolute long	x	
P.C. relative with offset	x	
P.C. relative with index	x	
Immediate	x	

Note that address register direct addressing cannot be used for byte-size operands.

Address Mode	Source	Destination
Data register direct	x	
Address register direct		
Address register indirect		x

Address Mode	Source	Destination
Postincrement register indirect		x
Predecrement register indirect		x
Register indirect with offset		x
Register indirect with index		x
Absolute short		x
Absolute long		x
P.C. relative with offset		
P.C. relative with index		
Immediate		

C and X are set if a borrow is generated, cleared otherwise. N is set if the result is negative, cleared otherwise. V is set if an overflow occurs, cleared otherwise. Z is set if the result is zero, cleared otherwise.

SUBTRACT ADDRESS
Mnemonic – SUBA

This is a special form of SUB using an address register as the destination operand.

Address Mode	Source	Destination
Data register direct	x	
Address register direct	x	x
Address register indirect	x	
Postincrement register indirect	x	
Predecrement register indirect	x	
Register indirect with offset	x	
Register indirect with index	x	
Absolute short	x	
Absolute long	x	
P.C. relative with offset	x	
P.C. relative with index	x	
Immediate	x	

If a word source data is specified instead of long-word, it will be sign-extended prior to the subtraction.

Note that unlike SUB, no flags are affected by SUBA.

79

SUBTRACT IMMEDIATE
Mnemonic – SUBI

This instruction subtracts immediate data from the destination operand.

Address Mode	Source	Destination
Data register direct		x
Address register direct		x
Address register indirect		x
Postincrement register indirect		x
Predecrement register indirect		x
Register indirect with offset		x
Register indirect with index		x
Absolute short		x
Absolute long		x
P.C. relative with offset		
P.C. relative with index		
Immediate	x	

The data size can be specified as byte, word or long-word. If byte-size is specified, the low-order (second) byte of the immediate data word is used.

SUBTRACT QUICK
Mnemonic – SUBQ

This is a special version of immediate-addressing subtraction for small operands (1 to 8).

Address Mode	Source	Destination
Data register direct		x
Address register direct		x
Address register indirect		x
Postincrement register indirect		x
Predecrement register indirect		x
Register indirect with offset		x
Register indirect with index		x
Absolute short		x

Address Mode	Source	Destination
Absolute long		x
P.C. relative with offset		
P.C. relative with index		
Immediate	x	

Note that address register direct addressing cannot be used if the operand size is byte.

The effect on flags is the same as for SUB.

SUBTRACT WITH EXTEND
Mnemonic – SUBX

This instruction subtracts both the source data and the value of the X flag from the destination data.

This instruction can use either register direct addressing or address register indirect addressing, but both operands must use the same mode. Thus it can be used for register-to-register or memory-to-memory subtraction.

When address register indirect addressing is used, both address registers are decremented before the operation. This facilitates multiple-precision arithmetic.

For the effect on the flags see SBCD.

SWAP REGISTER HALVES
Mnemonic – SWAP

This instruction exchanges the most significant 16 bits of a register with the least significant 16 bits.

The N flag will be set to the value of bit 31 after the swap. The Z flag will be set if the register contains zero. C and V are always cleared, and X is not affected.

INDIVISIBLE TEST AND SET
Mnemonic – TAS

This instruction tests a byte of data in the destination operand,

and sets the N and Z flags accordingly. It then sets the MSB of the destination data to 1. This operation cannot be interrupted.

Address Mode	Source	Destination
Data register direct		x
Address register direct		
Address register indirect		x
Postincrement register indirect		x
Predecrement register indirect		x
Register indirect with offset		x
Register indirect with index		x
Absolute short		x
Absolute long		x
P.C. relative with offset		
P.C. relative with index		
Immediate		

The C and V flags are always cleared, X is not affected.

TRAP
Mnemonic – TRAP

Initiates exception processing. The program counter is incremented to point to the next instruction, then saved on the system stack, followed by the current contents of the status register. Program execution then continues at an address obtained from the exception vector table.

A full description of this instruction and of exception processing is beyond the scope of this introductory book.

TRAP ON OVERFLOW
Mnemonic – TRAPV

This instruction will initiate exception processing if the V flag is set when it is executed.

TEST AN OPERAND
Mnemonic — TST

This instruction tests the destination operand, and sets the N and Z flags accordingly. The destination data is not altered.

Address Mode	Source	Destination
Data register direct		x
Address register direct		
Address register indirect		x
Postincrement register indirect		x
Predecrement register indirect		x
Register indirect with offset		x
Register indirect with index		x
Absolute short		x
Absolute long		x
P.C. relative with offset		
P.C. relative with index		
Immediate		

C and V are always cleared. X is not affected.

UNLINK
Mnemonic — UNLK

This instruction undoes the effect of a LINK instruction by loading the system stack pointer with the contents of a specified address register. This address register is then loaded with a long word pulled from the stack. See the description of the LINK instruction.

Chapter 4

STORAGE AND EXECUTION

Finding a place to store machine code, where it will not be corrupted by the operations of the computer, is a problem in most machines, and especially so with the Sinclair QL.

The Sinclair QL has a sophisticated operating system called QDOS. At the time of writing, full documentation on QDOS is not available, but from what has been published it is known that it is a multi-tasking time-sharing system for programs at the machine-code level. This means it is capable of apparently running two or more programs at once, though in fact it does this by executing a few instructions in one program, then a few in another, and so on — hence 'time-sharing'.

The operating system controls the whole of RAM, re-allocating areas as required. Care has to be taken when manipulating memory directly with POKE not to interfere with areas being used as buffers, as this can cause loss of data.

Crude methods of storage, such as poking the code into a REM statement at the beginning of a BASIC program, are not appropriate on the QL, as the position of the start of the BASIC area is not fixed.

The safe way to store machine code is by reserving memory space in the area allocated for 'resident procedures'. This area is really intended for machine code routines which will, in effect, become parts of the SuperBASIC language, but it can be safely purloined for other purposes.

There is a SuperBASIC function to reserve space in this area, RESPR. The statement 'start=RESPR(40)' will reserve 40 bytes in this area, and put the address of the first byte in the SuperBASIC variable 'start'. This variable can be used to control the POKEing of machine code or data into memory.

It is also possible to load and run machine code programs in the 'transient programs' area of memory, provided they meet the QDOS requirements for multitasking. This means they must use fully position-independent code, and have their own space for data, stack, etc. Such programs can be loaded and run from BASIC using EXEC.

The only statement for executing a machine-code routine from within a SuperBASIC program is 'CALL'. SuperBASIC has no USR statement. CALL is followed by the start address of the routine, and then up to 13 optional parameters, which are loaded into the 68008's internal registers (from D0 to D7, then A0 to A5 in sequence).

When using CALL, the use of register A6 is reserved for the operating system. Before returning to BASIC, using RTS, register D0 must be set to 0 using MOVEQ 0,D0. If this is not done, program execution will halt on return with an error message.

Of course, if only very short, simple routines are involved, and the computer is not being asked to do anything else at the same time, liberties can be taken, as is the case with the demonstration routines which complete this chapter.

Programs

The three demonstration programs given here are only intended as a very simple introduction to QL machine code, and are not intended to be practical machine code programs. They enable you to run some machine code programs so that you can see some 68008 routines in operation, and can try out a few 68008 instructions. They are written in a form that makes them relatively easy to follow, and machine code programs would not normally be entered and run in this rather crude way. In fact, as pointed out in previous chapters, it is probably best to avoid true machine code routines altogether and to use assembly language. The problem with using machine code on a 68008 computer is the time taken to calculate the instruction code numbers. Although the 68008 has just 56 instructions, there are numerous variations on most of these. Thus it is not simply a matter of looking up the code number for each instruction, but it is instead a matter of working out the state of each of the 16 bits in the binary code number, and then converting this to a decimal number that can be entered into the program. This is a very slow and impractical process, and is also one that is likely to produce errors. We have therefore not included details on how to work out the code number for each instruction and every variation, and have made the reasonable assumption that you will use an assembler for any code programs that you write.

PROGRAM 1
Addition

```
  5 CLS
 10 POKE_W 200000,12348
 20 INPUT a:POKE_W 200002,a
 30 POKE_W 200004,53372
 40 INPUT b:POKE_W 200006,b
 50 POKE_W 200008,13248
 60 POKE_L 200010,200050
 70 POKE_W 200014,28672
 80 POKE_W 200016,20085
 90 CALL 200000
100 PRINT PEEK_W(200050)
```

The first program takes two 16-bit numbers and adds them together. Line 5 clears the screen and then line 10 POKEs a 16-bit instruction code to address 200000. This is the start address of the routine, and the first instruction moves the immediate data to register D0. Line 20 is used to input the first number in the calculation and to then POKE this to address 200002. Note that as the data and instructions are 16 bits long they occupy two 8-bit memory locations. Hence the instruction is actually at addresses 200000 and 200001, and the immediate data is at addresses 200002 and 200003. Also, the POKE-W (POKE word) version of the POKE instruction has to be used.

Line 30 POKEs an instruction code to address 200004, and this one adds the immediate data to register D0. The immediate data (the second number in the calculation) is entered into the computer and written to the appropriate pair of addresses at line 40. The answer to the calculation will be in register D0, and it must be transferred from here to somewhere in memory so that it can be PEEKed and

86

printed on screen. Line 50 is a move instruction, and it transfers the contents of D0 to the absolute address in the following four bytes. A POKE-L (POKE long word) instruction is used to place the address in the appropriate four memory locations. This is at line 60 and the address is 200050. Lines 70 and 80 provide the MOVEQ 0,D0 and RTS instructions which hand control back to the operating system.

Of course, the program has so far only POKEd the program and data into memory, and a CALL instruction (line 90) is needed in order to run the machine code. Finally, line 100 PEEKs the answer and prints it on screen. When running the program remember to keep the numbers within the 16-bit limit (i.e. 65535 or less), and that the program does not take into account any carry.

PROGRAM 2
Subtraction

```
  5 CLS
 10 POKE_W 200000,12348
 20 INPUT a:POKE_W 200002,a
 30 POKE_W 200004,36988
 40 INPUT b:POKE_W 200006,b
 50 POKE_W 200008,13248
 60 POKE_L 200010,200050
 70 POKE_W 200014,28672
 80 POKE_W 200016,20085
 90 CALL 200000
100 PRINT PEEK_W(200050)
```

The second program works in much the same way as the first one, but the add immediate instruction code is replaced by the one for the subtract immediate instruction. The program therefore provides subtraction of the second number from the first, but as we are using the unsigned version of the subtract instruction you must use a second number that is smaller than the first.

PROGRAM 3
Multiplication

```
10 CLS
20 POKE_W 200000,12348
30 INPUT a
33 POKE_W 200002,a
40 POKE_W 200004,49404
50 INPUT b:POKE_W 200006,b
60 POKE_W 200008,9152
70 POKE_L 200010,200050
80 POKE_W 200014,28672
90 POKE_W 200016,20085
100 CALL 200000
110 PRINT PEEK_L(200050)
```

Multiplication is provided by the third program, but this differs slightly from the previous two programs in that the result of the calculation can be up to 32 bits long. Thus a PEEK-L (PEEK long word) instruction is used to print out the answer. With 32 bits available the answer can be a very large number indeed, but remember that the QL displays such numbers in scientific notation.